Corn

by Lisa Trumbauer

Consultant: Jerry Lindeen,
Iowa Farmer: Corn and Soybeans

for early readers

Yellow Umbrella Books are published by Red Brick Learning
7825 Telegraph Road, Bloomington, Minnesota 55438
http://www.redbricklearning.com

Editorial Director: Mary Lindeen
Senior Editor: Hollie J. Endres
Senior Designer: Gene Bentdahl
Photo Researcher: Signature Design
Developer: Raindrop Publishing
Consultant: Jerry Lindeen, Iowa Farmer: Corn and Soybeans
Conversion Assistants: Jenny Marks, Laura Manthe

Library of Congress Cataloging-in-Publication Data
Trumbauer, Lisa, 1963-
  Corn / by Lisa Trumbauer
     p. cm.
  Includes index.
  ISBN 0-7368-5846-6 (hardcover)
  ISBN 0-7368-5276-X (softcover)
  1. Corn—Juvenile literature. I. Title. II. Series.
  SB191.M2T78 2005
  632.1'5—dc22
                                          2005016138

Photo Credits:
Cover and Title Page: Corel; Page 2: Barbara Bannister; Gallo Images/Corbis; Page 3: PhotoDisc Images; Page 4: North Wind Picture Archives, (inset) Photodisc/Cartesia; Page 5: North Wind Picture Archives; Page 6: Bettmann/Corbis; Page 7: Corbis; Page 8: Tony Arruza/Corbis; Page 9: Douglas Kirkland/Corbis; Page 10: DK Images; Page 11: Corbis; Page 12: Macduff Everton/Corbis; Page 13: Ariadne van Zandbergen/Images of Africa; Page 14: Chuck Pefley/Alamy

1 2 3 4 5 6 11 10 09 08 07 06

Table of Contents

A Tasty Surprise

Look at these plants. They are huge! They tower over 8 feet (3.05 m) tall. Do you see the big leaves?

The leaves are called **husks**. If you peel back the husks, you'll see the yellow **kernels** of corn inside. The kernels grow on an inner core, called a **cob**.

A Plant of the Americas

The Americas

People ate corn thousands of years ago in the Americas. First, corn grew wild. Then Native Americans learned how to grow it. They called it **maize**.

Corn became a very important food for the Native Americans. They thought of many ways to cook corn. Native Americans knew that when heated, some types of kernels popped. We still eat popcorn today!

When Europeans first came (to) America, they had never heard about corn. The Native Americans showed the European settlers how to plant and **harvest** corn. Corn was served at (the) first Thanksgiving.

Corn quickly became popular with the European settlers in America. More and more farmers began planting this crop. Soon corn became an important food to the settlers, too.

How Do We Use Corn Today?

Today, corn has many uses. Farmers use a lot of the corn they grow to feed their animals, or livestock.

People also eat sweet corn. The corn you buy in the grocery store may come on the cob, in a can, or frozen. No matter how it comes, it is healthy to eat.

Have you ever had corn chips or corn cereal? Both are made with corn. Cornmeal is ground-up corn. People use cornmeal in many ways, including to make corn bread.

Some corn is made into a sweet liquid called **corn syrup**. You can find corn syrup in juices and sodas. Corn is also used to make some things we don't eat, like garbage bags and drinking straws!

Planting and Harvesting

Corn is planted in the spring. The corn plant grows throughout the summer. It grows taller and taller. **Ears** begin to grow on the stalk. Corn silk comes out of the top of the ears.

The tassels at the top of the cornstalk have **pollen**. The pollen falls on the silk. Each piece of silk will grow a kernel of corn. By fall, the corn is ready to be harvested. The corn silk is brown and dry, but the kernels inside the husk are ripe and juicy.

Farmers harvest the corn. You can buy the corn in the store or at a farmers' market. Today corn is enjoyed by people all around the world.

Glossary

cob—the middle part of an ear of corn on which corn kernels grow

corn syrup—a sweetener made from corn

ear—the part of a corn plant where the seeds grow

harvest—to pick or gather a crop

husk—the part of a plant that covers the fruit or the seeds

kernel—a grain or seed, especially of corn

maize—corn; the corn plant.

pollen—needed for some parts of a plant to grow

Index

Word Count: 401
Early-Intervention Level: L